To: Amy

Crown Me

Poems, Songs, & quotes

By
Symone Barnes

You are beautiful
You are Strong
Stay Crowned!

Crown Me

Printed in the United States of America
Powered by Bookemon. www.bookemon.com

ISBN 978- 163625372-5

This book is dedicated to the Queens
and Kings in my Kingdom

You know who you are.

To all that are still standing wearing
your crown, claiming your throne.

Dear Queen,

Smile, because the strength within you
shall grow.
Laugh, because the pain will only feed
your glow.
Empower yourself, because you have
your freedom to say NO.
Don't ever compromise your kingdom,
Let Go.
They can never take your ***CROWN***, only
you can remove it.
Some will never bow down, but you will
ALWAYS be ROYAL; Choose it.

-Symone Barnes

FIND ME

FIND ME,
        BECAUSE I DO NOT HIDE
SEE ME
        BECAUSE I DO NOT CRY
HEAR ME
        MY SILENCE IS MY VOICE
RELEASE ME
BECAUSE DEPRESSION ALWAYS
HAS A CHOICE
                FIND ME.

-Symone Barnes

Wasted Time

I hate myself for wanting more
for believing in the after and
not seeing what it was before.
I never believed in magic but
damn what we had was pretty close.
Until I finally saw your painting and
your true colors started to show.
As you looked into my eyes
I embraced your lies.
Realizing who you really were.

-Symone Barnes

Wishes

I wish you were blind
So, you are eager to hear.

I wish you lost someone
So, you realize whose here.

I wish you had no lungs
So, maybe you learn to rely on your
heart.

I wish you had no memory
So, you have to learn who you are.

I wish you had little strength
So, you find that you are really weak.

I wish you had no feet
So, you believe in falling to your knees.

I wish you had no truth
So, you get tired of telling me lies.

I wish I had no wish
So, then maybe you wouldn't have
broke mine.

-Symone Barnes

True Glow

My skin,

My beauty,

My essence,

My truth, without the foundation of

coverage are you comfortable with you?

-Symone Barnes

Find the future
Thank the past
Leave behind the damage,
It only keeps you chained,
Your key is your mind
Your heart is your destiny,
Empty the fear
Believe in the test
Design yourself to lead.
The strong are the blessed.

Truth is….

You're all I chose to know

Truth is….

Time apart is to really let go

Truth is….

It's time to face the real

Truth is….

The memories of us can only be the
past in order for our futures to heal

Truth is….

There was really no truth

Truth is….

I'm always lying to myself when I say
that I need you.

-Symone Barnes

She has dominion
She has power
She has authority
She is free

When she cries her weakness dies.

To: LIFE NOW
From: MY NEXT LIFE

Love cautiously without doubt in
yourself.

Empty your fears for they won't be
allowed here.

Forgive what shallowness may break
your heart.

Understand to accept the end, to
embrace the start.

Learn the message of half of goodbye to
experience the wholeness of hello.

Pain is only heavy until you pursue the
power of "Let go".

Wear your imperfections perfectly
because what's hidden won't exist.

Only keep what you really have because
what you never did you can't miss.

-Symone Barnes

I'm Free

Her skin was burned
Her mind was learned
They wanted the "best" for her
So, they kept her freedoms
Buried her decisions
Stripped her choice.
For years she was lost, still in her mind.
Until she ran to reach her voice.
Something they thought she'd never
find.

Smiles

I smile because I'm blessed
I wake up and I can say "What's next?"

I smile because I'm me
No one knows what's it like to be within
myself and yet still be free.

I smile because I am weird
Complacency is my only fear.

I smile because this world has so much
to give and here, I am ready to embrace.

I smile because I still endure love in this
world of hate.

I smile because I stand yet the ground
beneath me feels like falling.

I smile because I am an Instrument of
Freedom and I accept my calling.

I Smile.

No Tomorrow

We are not promised Tomorrow
We are promised Now
Now to live
Now to accept
Now to fall
Now to dream
We are not promised Tomorrow
We are promised Now
Now to impact
Now to change
Now to love
Now to see
We are not promised Tomorrow
We are promised Now
Now to reach

-Symone Barnes

Chains are going to always bind your
happy.
Make your piece of mind not exist.
But the key is within
Unlock, Unfold, Embrace your own,
And live.

-Symone Barnes

Forgive

How could you lie
And still expect the truth?
How could you ever think you deserve
me when you know you're you?
How could you exist on this Earth with
a soul not Godly?
How can you hold up your head of
failure and fault so proudly?
How can you act and talk tall with a
mind that is so small?
But most of all,
How can you hurt someone that only
cared?
That never wanted anything but just to
see you there.

The Emptiness I feel for you can never
be filled again.
Tears of weakness I released from
myself, will never be wept for you
again.
I am not Weak enough to still **love you.**
I am Strong enough not to **hate you**.

Thank you for being sorry.
Thank you for not calling.
Thank you for pain and hurt that I know
I can live through. Your existence is no
longer relevant but **I Forgive You**.

Wish List

More time to live
More time to grieve
For beauty not to be priced
For souls to be free
For love to be real
True without feel
For voices to be heard
Lies to not burn
For money to lose its power
Save love before we're quick to devour

For Equality to really have won
For man to surrender his gun

Give me a wish
Show me a shooting star
Against all odds
Can reality and dreams really be so far?

Limitless
Opinionated
Vain
Envied

-Symone Barnes

Distance

We hate distance because
we long to be so close

We desire distance because vulnerability
is harder to show

We envy distance because of the fight
given to reach it

We lose distance because we forget
when we leave it

We appreciate distance because our
pains can be left behind

But distance is dangerous because we
are distant in anguish

Because distance is dependent on time

First Love

Thinking about you is like breathing in
flame
Thinking about you penetrates my
passion
I feel so much it enchants me away until
I snap back into reality
What just happened?
I know what did
Your cherished commitments and
lavished lies fooled a kid
Your tenderness that relished my heart
Yearned for something more
Vacationing away from my youth to the
Island of Grown we explored
I cried to sanitize my soul for your love
is what made me whole
To pretend, to avoid, to move on always
drenched my thirst
I'd dream you were my last
But all you'll ever compel to is my first

Dear Society

I am beautiful
I am strong
I am different

You plaster your criticism based on what you see
Neglect our individualism
Try to define our empowerment
To contain our free
Send us sex to corrupt our success

Promote get lit with vape or a fix
Making it convenient to accept the labels men pamper us with
Sluts, thots, these hoes well NO!
Women, girls are so much more
Alienated once before

We were designed to shine, run the world, to create a dream to sore
So keen with the word weak but feast off of our defeat

As we walk through judgements that burn like fire
Crucifying man that denies a HER to hire
Dear Society, I aspire

BROKEN LOVE HEALS

My Soul is **Black.**
My heart is cracked.
And the worst part is- you know that.
Yet so you love me over
A love that should be **Over**
Until we're forced in addiction
Never finding **Sober.**
This is the love I know.
This is the love that feeds me pain so I can grow.
This love is my beauty.
This love is my scar.

We are broken
But we love past what we are.

Don't Leave.

I won't be **silent**
I won't be **quiet**

I won't **back down**
I will not **give up**

Underestimate me more
I haven't had **enough.**

-Symone Barnes

A Glance

The way you stare
Made you easy to see
Every time our eyes meet
Our connection is brief
You said I didn't know you
Guarantee I know those eyes
They look at me and respect the
chance I won't give
At core your sworn with lies

-Symone Barnes

Why can't we smile when we are
sad?
If pain only makes us stronger
Then what really derives us to be
mad?

-Symone Barnes

Who am I alone?
Who are we on our own?
Why should I move on?
When feeling different feels the
same.
When I constantly change.
Trying to run away from pain.

-Symone Barnes

Life is different
Time is gone
Pain has shifted
Left love to fall
Happiness to reveal
Hope to devour
Dreams to be wished on
I'm ready for God's shower
Resentment is scarce
Fear is forgotten
Anger is loosened
My Satan you're losing

-Symone Barnes

To the only F**boy I Ever Loved

Only love in my eyes
Just a long screw in theirs.
What's the truth behind "I miss
you" texts?
Never mind I don't really care
Because you text me, I still reply
Feel the truth but choose to
believe the lie.

When I love you I'm hurt.
But then I cut you off I'm worse.

You put a weight on my heart
That I can't seem to lift
The thought of forgetting all this
time
Feels like I'm falling off a cliff
I don't take back any of the
things we've done.
But I really do wish you weren't
the one.

I'm letting go of more than my
lust,
I'm leaving behind my trust.

Endless time won't be enough of
a high to deal with this coping.
Meanwhile deep in my soul
I'll still be hoping.

After all this we can never be
"just friends".
Thank you for leaving me with
just myself to have again.

I'll set my own self free
No one can tell me who they think I
should be
And I'll love until I can't feel my heart
I'll live my life
I'll **Live Me**

-Symone Barnes

We say we want peace for one another.
Yet we still point our guns at each other.

-Symone Barnes

Forgiving you is not what made me
stronger.
Coming to terms with the fact that I
never will,
Is what released you from me.

-Symone Barnes

It felt like I was failing
Until faith fought for me.
God was allowing me to be human
Knowing all along he would catch me
when I fall.

-Symone Barnes

It was never about liking the color of my
skin.
It is about **Respecting** it.
Where down the line did you get
confused?

-Symone Barnes

Your truth can be loud
Your youth can be proud
Never be apologetic for who you are.

-Symone Barnes

Don’t underestimate my power when
it’s quiet
My silence is violent.

-Symone Barnes

We lose ourselves in happiness.
We always find ourselves in pain.

-Symone Barnes

What are you in this world of worth
without your word?

-Symone Barnes

DOMESTIC LOVE

This is never
This is it will get better
This is the outside looking in
This is the reason why we don't quit
Maybe I shouldn't stay
But my heart won't leave
Nobody understands what's within this fein
Don't compel this strength to weak
Don't judge these scars just see
This passionate pain, fear, trust is beyond us
Welcome to our DOMESTIC LOVE

It hurts to say the truth
It pains to feel like I choose you
But in reality, I'm choosing me
This inevitable feeling that makes me feel enough
This DOMESTIC LOVE

I am imagining smiles
I am dreaming happiness
I am smelling the potential of right love
But all I am tasting is this DOMESTIC LOVE

El sonido de la luz yo siempre etoy aquí
Pero parece que solo veo miedo
El sonido de la libertad se escapa de mis oídos
¿Por qué está todo tan frío?
El sonido de los disparos es como la ira responde
¿Cómo dejamos que el dolor se hiciera tan grande?
Estos son el sonido de la vida
Es hora de cambia estos sonidos

Actually She Can.
Because she failed, fell, and made
mistakes in order to do so.

-Symone Barnes

Truth is deep when it is naked and not
covered.
But truth is never accepted until a lie is
discovered.
Never love yourself undercover.
You are not weak for not wanting to be
alone.
People are more than experiences, they
are steppingstones to your blessings, to
YOUR top.
You are never lost when you need to
find yourself.
You are your key to your lock.

-Symone Barnes

Laws of A Woman

I am Matter.

You cannot create me.
You cannot destroy me.

I am made from everything around me.

I am strength when I fail.
I am my ground when I fall.
I am my yes when I am denied.

I am a Woman of Color when I am
defined.

I Am Matter.

-Symone Barnes

Never allow your mentality to be stuck.

A blind man can lead.

A healed wound can bleed.

Change is free.

Black Power founded by love and common good will always be bigger.

Not every human in a uniform behind a badge, pulls the trigger.

You are entitled to curves of story and weight of history to be a perfect figure.

Anyone is welcome to leave you when you don't need them.

Man will never let hate succeed him.

Love only belongs to freedom.

-Symone Barnes

Black belongs here.
Indian belongs here.
Latino belongs here.
Asian belongs here.
White belongs here.

Color belongs here.

-Symone Barnes

Estoy bailando libertad.

Estoy bailando belleaza.

Estoy bailando fuerte.

Estoy bailando intelligencia

Estoy bailando poder.

Estoy bailando realeza.

Estoy bailando con mi corona.

-Symone Barnes

Progress our rights.
Express our rights.
Access our rights.
Stress our rights.

Protests our rights.
Protect our rights.
Neglect our rights.
Respect our rights

-Symone Barnes

You do not have to **Break** the
Law,
To **Change** the Law.

-Symone Barnes

It’s essential that you realize…
If he leaves you
You lose nothing.

But when you leave him
You go back to winning.

-Symone Barnes

Time has made me a woman
Lies has made me a woman
Demise has made me a woman
Christ has made me a woman

Peers have made me a woman
Tears have made me a woman
Fears have made me a woman
Years have made me a woman

My pain has made me a woman
My gain has made me a woman
My name has made me a woman
My strength has made me a woman

-Symone Barnes

It is easy to love someone when they
love themselves.
They just don’t know care.
Know trust.
Know love.
But they know how to apply it.

-Symone Barnes

We cannot Possess our Possessions.
We must know what stays and what
goes.
We must separate the truth from what's
told.
We must know when to let go and when
to hold.
Never possess our Possessions.
A Possessed mind,
disrupts a successful grind.

-Symone Barnes

When did disrespect become so cute to
wear?
When did speaking the truth become an
option to share?
When did ignoring your worth become
tolerable to bare?
Nobody Cares.

When did becoming a follower make
you a leader?
When did the only way to feel strong
meant calling others weaker?
When did beauty only consists of
physical features?
Your purpose is deeper.

When did it become necessary to use
war to find peace?
When did we allow anger and hate to
lead?
When did we need others to starve in
order for some to feed?
Sometimes you have to silence your
mind to let your heart speak.

-Symone Barnes

Power
Evolution
Acceptance
Courage
Earned

-Symone Barnes

I AM STRONG FOREVER
NEVER GIVING UP
NEVER EVER GIVE UP
ALWAYS BE STRONG FOR YOUR
FAMILY
AND LOVE YOUR FAMILY

-Feature from Little King

I've been on my own all my life
Never have been afraid to cry
I'm the only one that fights my fears
I'm the only one that can dry these tears
I guess that's why they say I'm so
independent and strong
But in reality, there is no one to depend
on
It's safe with just Me, Myself, And I

-Symone Barnes

People are not your problems
People are your opportunity to be blessed
Never treat anyone less

-Symone Barnes

I believe so hard that every time I try it
just falls apart

-Symone Barnes

She lost her virginity
But she was still a virgin to intimacy.

-Symone Barnes

We are not **Boring** because we choose to respect ourselves.

We are not **Stuck up** because we don't choose to neglect ourselves.

We are not **Impossible** because we have goals and morals.

I guess Women are not built like this anymore huh.

-Symone Barnes

I never accepted who you were.
I always knew you could change.
It was years ago I let go of what
wouldn't happen.
Dreams together surrendered for closure
and yet still you remain.
What am I supposed to believe?
My mind screams while my heart
bleeds.
Being a hopeless romantic got me hurt.
Believing in love stole my worth.
But I still care.

Night

The dark sky reminds me of how late
you stayed.
The whispers in the wind reminds me of
the truth in each word you really meant.
The smell of aged cigarettes reminds me
of the toxicity I yet seem to miss.
It's only at Night I relive our kiss.
It's only at Night my heart is submiss to
the thoughts of you.

-Symone Barnes

Sometimes you will need to **Break** your
life in order to **Save** your life.

Break stipulations
Break trends
Break rules
Breakthrough for you.

-Symone Barnes

Who am I today?
Am I stupid or dumb?
Who am I today?
The pills or the gun?
Who am I today?
Numb or sleep?
Who am I today?
Worthless or low?
Who am I today?
I don't know.
The world already tattoos me.
And everything I love consumes me.
I'm becoming something more than suicide.
Voiceless in my own mind.
Peace falls from my eyes and puts me to bed as I lie waiting for the next day, I question
Who am I?

No one is going to love you like you
No one is going to care the way you do
You cannot expect the world to
understand.
You can only hope someone will listen.
And when they do **Be Loud.**

-Symone Barnes

Let your Soul and your Spirit be best friends.

-Symone Barnes

Power to **You**
Power to **Me**
Power to **Us**
Power to **We**
Power to **See**
Power to **Be**
Power to **Greed**
Power "**I'm Free**"

-Symone Barnes

Tap into you.
Empower yourself.
Build a beautiful mind.
Practice peace.
Accept yourself.
Respect yourself
Inspire your empire.

-Symone Barnes

The Struggle becomes real when Hustle
is the only meal.

-Symone Barnes

Sometimes you have to refrain from
always saying sorry.
Allow yourself to feel and own up to
what may disturb others but brings you
peace.

-Symone Barnes

Curly Queen
Straight Queen
Silk Queen
Coarse Queen
Long Queen
Short Queen
Braided Queen
Shaved Queen

Your hair is one of your many crowns

Wear it proudly
Wear it boldly
Wear it fiercely
Wear it powerfully

Find I'm Possible within impossible
Give birth to your dreams
You are unstoppable

King you can cry
You are still strong inside

Queen you are strong
Respect yourself
You will still belong

Protect your essence
Your Mind is your weapon
Learn your lessons
Every pain becomes a healed blessing

Put power in your presence
Weak voices will lessen
You can succeed from behind
And still you are not second

Some will stay solid
Others will turn
Wisdom you receive
Strength you earn

I am my successor
Valued beyond measure
My Soul is forever
I am my ancestors.

I learned how to love you without wanting you.

Thus, the length of my cropped shirt
Lesson my worth and my sacredness

Respect me

Jeans that embrace my curves do not
permit your eyes to neglect me

What I wear
Is not
What I'm Worth

-Symone Barnes

She was both wild and free

She was both woman and war

She was both peaceful and voiceful

She was both happy and joyful

-Symone Barnes

A long way we have come.
A long way we have to go.

A lot we have revealed
A lot still left to show.

Afraid to be naked
Tired of what's taken
Forgetting my purpose
Like I misplaced it
So close to my anointment
So, the attacks get harder
In this world of sin, I still belong to you
Father
I am still navigating
Feels excruciating
Sometimes intimidating
Yet still very motivating
What will hurt me first?
My skin or my worth
In this world of need
In these times of greed
My heart bleeds
Feeling like the last potential seed

Give me strength to dream
Give me strength to see
Give me strength to breed

Mentality you have to free

Queen you are powerful

Queen you are cultural

Queen you are ancestral

Queen you are color

Queen you are crowned

-Symone Barnes

When we reform blue
When will we reform black?

When will we save our youth?
Give them time to see age
Give them truth and respect
Not a gun to take another's
breath

When will we put our history to
test?
When will we stand as one, so
we won't have to say, "I'm not like the
rest"?

When will we stop using our
pain as an excuse to cause more pain?
When will we use their hate as
ambition?
Success and achievement our
new ammunition

When will we push our people
without hidden jealousy?
Pursue our dreams to give
another theirs
Reduce the felonies
Produce more legacies

Made with strength
Made to challenge
Blessed with skin that armors us
for the battles we have won
Yes, we are "Woke"
With a strategy rooted from
mentality
Change has just begun

Do not fall for the enemy’s
attack
When will we reform?
Before the conform black

Congratulations!!! Crown Yourself Queen and/or King for reading this book and allowing it to bring comfort and confidence; allowing yourself to overcome emotions, obstacles, and all that comes with being an empowered person. Poetry is a beauty that everyone can share. I have dedicated 10 pages for you, not only to express your thoughts, but also to Crown your thoughts. Write what you feel raw and real and own it, because it's what allows us to feel free and powerful.

Thank you and get ready to crown yourself!

Crown Your Thoughts

Crown Your Thoughts

Crown Your Thoughts

Crown Your Thoughts

Crown Your Thoughts

Crown Your Thoughts

Crown Your Thoughts

Crown Your Thoughts

Crown Your Thoughts

Crown Your Thoughts

Made in the USA
Monee, IL
11 June 2021

71010485R00056